Children's Worship Activities

Year 3

Abingdon Press

Children's Worship Activities

Year 3

Copyright © 2003 by Abingdon Press

All rights reserved.

Permission is hereby granted to the purchaser of one copy of
Children's Worship Activity Sheets, Year 3
to reproduce copies of these pages for use in the local church.

ISBN 0-687-02818-3

Scripture quotations in this publication, unless otherwise indicated, are from the New Revised Standard Version of the Bible, copyrighted © 1989 by the Division of Christian Education of the National Council of the Churches of Christ in the United States of America, and are used by permission. All rights reserved.

Scripture quotations identified as Good News Translation are from the Good News Translation in Today's English Version—Second Edition. Copyright © 1992 American Bible Society. Used by permission.

03 04 05 06 07 08 09 10 11 12- 10 9 8 7 6 5 4 3 2 1

MANUFACTURED IN THE UNITED STATES OF AMERICA

"Joy" Stained Glass Window

Directions: Color the picture. Dip your cotton ball in the dish of oil. Spread it lightly over the back of the paper. Lay it aside on another sheet of paper to dry. Punch a hole in the top center to place yarn through in order to hang it at a window.

The Christian Year

Seasons	Celebrations

Advent
Begins four Sundays before Christmas
Colors: Purple or blue

A season of anticipation and preparation for the coming of Jesus

Christians remember and celebrate
- the prophets' words about the Messiah;
- the stories of Mary and Joseph as they learned they would be Jesus' parents;
- the trip to Bethlehem.

Christmas
Christmas Day through January 5
Colors: White or gold

A season of joy that begins with Christmas Day

Christians remember and celebrate
- Jesus' birth;
- the proclamation of good news to all people.

The Epiphany
January 6, twelve days after Christmas
Color: White or gold

A season for remembering that the Good News of the Messiah's birth is for all people

Christians celebrate
- the visit of the wise men;
- Jesus' baptism;
- the beginning of Jesus' ministry;
- Jesus as "the light of the world."

The Season After Epiphany
January 7 through the day before Ash Wednesday
Color: Green

Lent
Ash Wednesday through the Saturday before Easter (40 days, not including Sundays, which are days of celebration)
Color: Purple

A season of repentance and preparation for Easter

Christians remember and celebrate
- Jesus' forty days of fasting at the beginning of his ministry;
- Jesus' arrival in Jerusalem on Palm Sunday;
- Jesus' teachings in Jerusalem;
- Jesus' last supper with his disciples;
- Jesus' suffering and death.

Easter
Begins on Easter Sunday and continues until the day before Pentecost
Colors: White or gold

A season of joy and celebration

Christians remember
- the Resurrection;
- the days Jesus spent with the disciples after the Resurrection;
- the Ascension.

Day of Pentecost
Fifty days after Easter
Color: Red

A season to focus on what it means to be the people of God in the world today

The Season After Pentecost or Ordinary Time
After the Day of Pentecost until the beginning of Advent
Color: Green

Christians live in Ordinary Time as they
- remember the coming of the Holy Spirit;
- celebrate the beginning of the Christian church;
- proclaim the Good News;
- grow in discipleship;
- spread the message of living as Jesus taught.

NAZARETH TO BETHLEHEM MAZE

Gifts for Jesus

Directions: Look at each symbol with a line above it. Look at the top of the page and find the matching angle with a letter in it. Copy the letter on the line below that has the same angle below it.

Grid 1: S T L / D A J / M H E
Grid 2 (X-shape): F, O, I, N
Grid 3 (circle): U, Y

What Can I Do For Jesus?

Jesus said, "J U _ _   _ _   _ _ _

_ _ _   _ _   _ _   _ _ _   _ _

_ _ _   _ _ _ _ _   _ _   _ _ _ _ _

_ _ _   _ _ _   _ _   _ _."

8

Copyright © 2003 Abingdon Press. Permission is granted for the original purchaser to reproduce this activity for use in a local church setting. Copyright © 2000 Abingdon Press.

FiND THe HiDDeN iTeMS

Can you find a teddy bear, a stuffed elephant, a baby bottle, and a rattle?

Angles on Angels

Here are some facts from the Bible about angels. Find and read each verse and fill in the blanks. The correct answers are scrambled after each verse. How is your angel knowledge?

Psalm 103:20 Bless the LORD, O you his angels, you _____ ones who do his _____. gyhmit ddgiibn

Revelation 10:1 And I saw another _____ angel coming down from heaven, wrapped in a cloud, with a _____ over his head; his face was like the ____, and his legs like _____ of fire. tihmgy brownia uns lraplis

Colossians 1:16 For in him all things in _____ and on _____ were created, things _____ and _____ ... all things have been created through him and for him. [This verse is talking about Jesus, and *everything* includes angels.] venahe rehat iiblsev iiibsvenl

Luke 16:22 The poor man died and was _____ away by the angels to be with _____. [Angels take us to heaven.] ridarce bhmarAa

Luke 15:10 Just so, I tell you, there is _____ in the _____ of the _____ of God over one sinner who _____. oyj seecnpre glesan perents

Hebrews 1:14 Are not all angels spirits in the divine _____, sent to _____ for the sake of those who are to inherit salvation? crivees vrees

Luke 1:26 In the sixth month the angel Gabriel was ____ by God to a town in Galilee called Nazareth. tsen

Luke 2:9-10 Then an angel of the Lord _____ before them, and the glory of the Lord shone around them, and they were terrified. But the angel ____ to them, "Do not be afraid." oodst dsia

Matthew 28:2 And suddenly there was a great earthquake; for an angel of the Lord, _____ from heaven, _____ and _____ back the stone and sat on it. sceeddgnni meac ldelro

Copyright © 2003 Abingdon Press. Permission is granted for the original purchaser to reproduce this activity for use in a local church setting.
Art: Robbie Short, © 2000 Abingdon Press.

1. Color the stained-glass window picture.
2. Use a cotton swab or small sponge to rub the picture with vegetable oil.
3. Make a frame from black construction paper. (The illustration suggests a shape.)
4. Add a piece of yarn or ribbon, and hang your picture in a window so that the light can shine through.

Copyright © 2003 Abingdon Press. Permission is granted for the original purchaser to reproduce this activity for use in a local church setting.
Art: Bob Jones, © 1994 Cokesbury.

How Many Ways Can You Say Merry Christmas?

Christians all over the world celebrate Christmas. Can you say "Merry Christmas" in several languages?

Froehliche Weihnachten
German

Joyeux Noel
French

Kilisimasi Fiefia
Tongan

God Jul
Swedish

Zalig Kerstfeest
Dutch

Feliz Navidad
Spanish

Can you remember the ways you learned to say *Peace* last quarter?

Getting Ready for a Baby

Directions: Read the Bible verse and write the word in the blank. Also write each word on the line near the point (see example). Each word appears twice. Line these words up across from each other and glue the pieces to another piece of paper. What do the pieces make?

I have said these things to you so that my _joy_ may be in you. John 15:11

joy

He gives the _____ to the faint, and strengthens _____ less. Isaiah 40:29

Ask and you will receive, so that your _____ may be complete. John 16:24

May the God of _____ fill you with all joy and peace in believing, so that you may abound in _____ by the power of the Holy Spirit. Romans 15:13

Finally, be strong in the Lord and in the strength of his _____. Ephesians 6:10

And let the _____ of Christ rule in your hearts. Colossians 3:15

But I will _____ continually, and will praise you yet more and more. Psalm 71:14

Let mutual _____ continue. Hebrews 13:1

I will both lie down and sleep in _____; for you alone, O LORD, make me lie down in safety. Psalm 4:8

Beloved, let us _____ one another, because _____ is from God. 1 John 4:7

A Royal Visitor

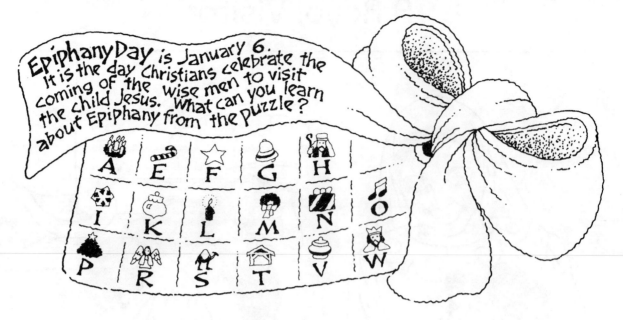

Epiphany Day is celebrated _ _ _ _ _ _ days after Christmas Day.

The word epiphany is a _ _ _ _ _ _ word that means _ _ _ _ _ _ _. Epiphany is a time for remembering that God has appeared to us in Jesus.

One of the symbols of Epiphany is the _ _ _ _ because it reminds us of the journey of the _ _ _ _ _ _ _ _ who came from the _ _ _ _ to find Jesus.

The wise men are sometimes called _ _ _ _ _ _ _ or _ _ _ _ _.

The worship paraments on Epiphany Day are _ _ _ _ _ _.

In some countries, _ _ _ _ _ are given on Epiphany Day to remember the visit of the wise men and God's _ _ _ _ _ of Jesus to all people.

Dove Mobiles

1. Trace the pattern and cut two dove shapes from construction paper.
2. Glue the two doves together with a ribbon or piece of yarn sandwiched between them. *Do not glue the wings!*
3. Fold the wings down so that the birds appear to fly.
4. Punch holes around the edge of a paper plate or a cardboard circle.
5. Use the ribbon or yarn to hang the birds at different lengths.
6. Punch two holes in the center of the circle and add a six-inch ribbon to use as a hanger.
7. Remember the dove that came to Jesus after his baptism.

Bible Verse Puzzle

	1	2	3	4	5
C	U	A	M	H	W
F	P	E	N	B	I
G	O	S	Y	V	J
K	R	T	L	D	X

<u>Y</u> <u>O</u> <u>U</u> <u>A</u> <u>R</u> <u>E</u> <u>M</u> <u>Y</u> <u>S</u> <u>O</u> <u>N</u>'

<u>T</u> <u>H</u> <u>E</u> <u>B</u> <u>E</u> <u>L</u> <u>O</u> <u>V</u> <u>E</u> <u>D</u>; <u>W</u> <u>I</u> <u>T</u> <u>H</u>

<u>Y</u> <u>O</u> <u>U</u> <u>I</u> <u>A</u> <u>M</u> <u>W</u> <u>E</u> <u>L</u> <u>L</u>

<u>P</u> <u>L</u> <u>E</u> <u>A</u> <u>S</u> <u>E</u> <u>D</u>.

Art: Mark James, © 2000 Abingdon Press.

I CAN MAKE GOOD CHOICES

Directions: Look at each pair of pictures below. Mark the circle that is the best choice.

Color the best-choice circles. Then cut them out.

Fold the tab over at the top of each picture and glue it to the back to form a loop.

Thread a piece of yarn through the loops to make a necklace. You may want to ask someone help you make big knots between the pictures.

Tie the ends of the strings together.

You have a necklace of good choices. Wear it home.

Copyright © 2003 Abingdon Press. Permission is granted for the original purchaser to reproduce this activity for use in a local church setting.
Art: Corbin Hilliam, © 2000 Abingdon Press.

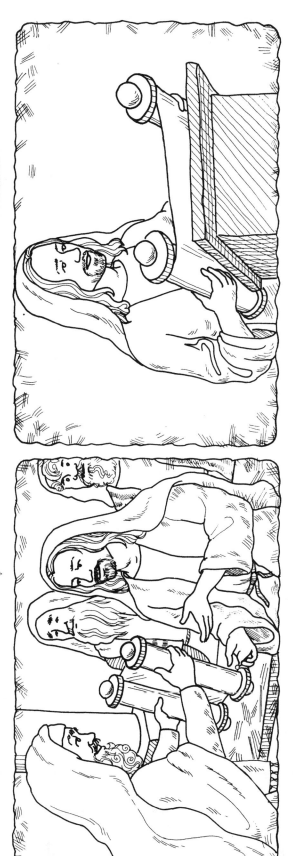
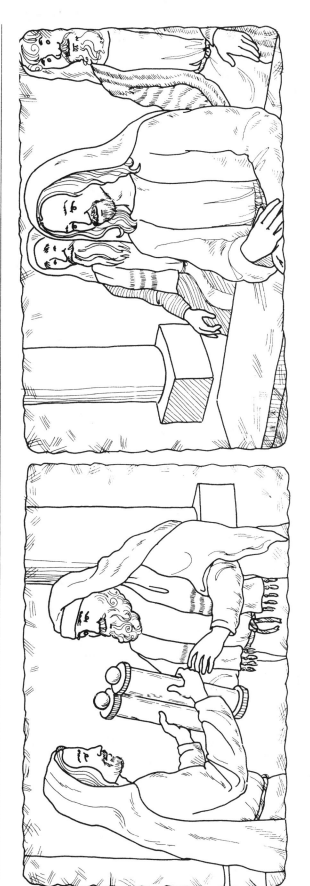

Jesus read from Isaiah: "The Spirit of the Lord... has anointed me to bring good news to the poor." (Luke 4:17-18, adapted)

Color in each space that does not contain one of the words from Luke 4:18:

The Spirit of the Lord is upon me, because he has anointed me to bring good news to the poor.

What word have you discovered? _____

Write some of your ideas about what this word means. _____

When Jesus called the first disciples,
"they left everything and followed him." (Luke 5:11b)
Draw a line to show the path each disciple can take to Jesus.

FISHING ON GALILEE

Fishing was a major industry in Galilee when Jesus lived there. Most of the fishing was done on the Sea of Galilee. Extended families owned a boat and worked together, usually for life.

Night was the best time for fishing. Burning torches attracted the fish to the surface of the water where the fisherman caught them in nets. A large net, equipped with weights to make it sink and floats to make it spread, was thrown out and then either pulled into the boat by hand or dragged to shore. Fish were stored in large baskets for their trip to the marketplace.

Many different kinds of fish were caught. Carp, sardines, mullet, and tilapia were considered to be "clean" and were eaten by the fishermen or sold to other Jews in the marketplace. The tilapia, which has a big mouth, is known today as Saint Peter's fish. Catfish, eel, and lamprey were "unclean" and were sold to non-Jews. Fish that were not eaten fresh were salted, pickled, or dried. Fish was quite cheap and along with bread was the mainstay of daily life.

Early Christians used the fish as an important symbol. The letters in the Greek word for *fish* are the first letters in the words *Jesus, Christ, God's Son, Savior*. The fish symbol is still used today as a reminder that Jesus said his followers would be fishers of people.

I Can Help

How can God use you?

Use a green crayon to circle the ways God could use you to do good.

Use a red crayon to cross out the things that you cannot do.

WORD FIND

DIRECTIONS: The words for the word find are in Luke 6:27-36. Draw a circle around each word and color in the circle. When you are finished, look for the word that the words spell.

FIND THESE WORDS:

ABUSE	COAT	LEND	SHIRT
BLESS	CREDIT	MERCIFUL	SINNERS
CHEEK	ENEMIES	REWARDS	STRIKES

```
M H S N O E Q O E Z U S M R Z I U S W L
E A E J S S H I R T S E E E O M I A O E
R R O A R T S T B W I C S W D A V I D S
C W I H W R E T J N N Z B M L U O A T H
I R T X N I C L R U N R O S A L Y N R S
F G E W J K B A A R E Y A O J D E K M C
U Y G R U E M S T Z R T E O N I N E E O
L E N D U S C O A T S Z L E W N P A R O
R S R N C L A G S L U E D A E G T N F P
E O S R A R B R U F W T C L R C H E E K
C N T A T Y A M H J G R I C E U S Q E S
A E E S P M S E N N E Q R B W J E M F I
K E O M Y P A A N D D E C T A B U S E N
O J J O I J S Y I Q A N E B R F R M S R
E N E L O E Y T A E M N V T D S P N L T
S R X M L Q S Y M V U K E V S B L E S S
```

Copyright © 2003 Abingdon Press. Permission is granted for the original purchaser to reproduce this activity for use in a local church setting.
Art: Doug Jones, © 2000 Abingdon Press.

Which pictures show children doing what God wants?

Which pictures show a promise you want to make to God?

Color the pictures you choose. Then cut them out and glue them to construction paper.

Ask a helper to print "I Will Obey God" at the top of your poster.

The Hebrew Scriptures Helped Jesus

Jesus knew the Scriptures and often used them to guide his actions or to teach others God's way. The Hebrew Scriptures that Jesus used were the same as our Old Testament today. Read the references below to discover times when the Scriptures helped Jesus. Match each reference with the circumstance in the right column.

Matthew 4:1-4	When Jesus identifies himself
Mark 7:5-7	When Jesus began his ministry
Luke 4:16-19	When Jesus was tempted
John 8:12	When Jesus rebuked the Pharisees

My Bible Helps Me

The Scriptures can help us every day. Match the references with some times when you need help. You will use both the Old Testament and the New Testament.

Exodus 20:12	When I am tempted to gossip about my friends
John 13:34	When I want to do something my parents forbid
Proverbs 3:5-6	When I don't feel like being friendly
James 4:11	When I cannot decide what to do

Jesus in the Wilderness

LIVING LENT

Have you ever heard someone say she is giving up a certain food for Lent? Usually anyone who does this is making an offering to God by not eating something he really enjoys, like pizza or chocolate. This idea comes from an old practice of going without eggs, butter, milk, sweets, and other foods during Lent. To sacrifice eating tasty foods is one way to honor Jesus' sacrifice of his life.

Ash Wednesday is the day when people stop eating certain foods, so on the day before, it was customary to use up all the butter, eggs, and sugar in the house. In some places this day is called Fat Tuesday. Another name is Pancake Tuesday. Pancake Tuesday has a history dating back hundreds of years and often featured a race through the town square with people carrying skillets and flipping pancakes three times before reaching the church steps. Perhaps churches in your community host pancake suppers to keep that tradition.

Family Fun: Start your own Pancake Tuesday tradition! Make pancakes for supper, but before eating, run a relay around the table. Place the first pancake in a lightweight skillet or on a paper plate. Spin the syrup bottle to see who starts, then that person will run around the table once, flip the pancake once, then hand it off to the person on the right. When everyone has had a turn, the winner is determined by who dropped the pancake the fewest times. This person wins and is served first at supper.

Copyright © 2003 Abingdon Press. Permission is granted for the original purchaser to reproduce this activity for use in a local church setting.
Art: Terry Sirrell, © 2000 Abingdon Press.

Valentine Card

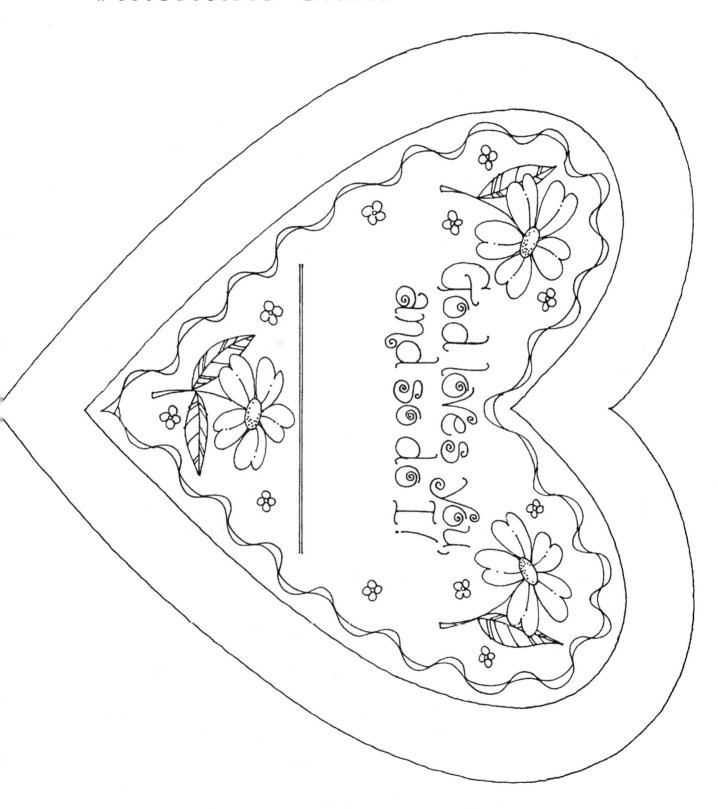

LIVING LENT #3

The four Gospels have many similarities, but they also have distinctive differences. Try to match up the books with correct information.

Read and Match

1. Matthew 1:1
2. Mark 1:1-3
3. Luke 1:1-4
4. John 1:1-5

a. an investigation
b. the divine origin of Christ
c. a genealogy
d. a prophecy

Remember and Match

1. Matthew
2. Mark
3. Luke
4. John

a. Which Gospel tells of the Christmas shepherds?
b. Which Gospel tells of the wise men?
c. Which Gospel uses the "I am" phrases?
d. Which Gospel has a shorter and longer ending?

Research, Recall, and Match

1. Matthew
2. Mark
3. Luke
4. John

a. Which book was written by a physician?
b. Which book has the most chapters?
c. Which book devotes half the work to Jesus' last eight days?
d. Who said that if all the things Jesus did were written down, the world couldn't contain all the books?

Jesus Worshiped—We Worship

DIRECTIONS: One side of the page shows pictures of worship in Jesus' day. On the other side of the page are pictures of worship in our day. Match the pictures by drawing a line from one to the other.

Disciple Acrostic

DIRECTIONS: The word *disciple* is vertical on the page. Think of a word that describes a disciple and has that letter in it. Print that word on the line. An example: For the letter D. A disciple *studies* the Bible. So you will print S T U D I E S. Do the same with each letter. Do not repeat a word.

D _ _ _ _ _ _
_ _ S _ _ _ _
_ _ C _ _ _ _
_ _ _ P _ _ _
_ _ L _ _ _ _
_ _ E _ _ _ _

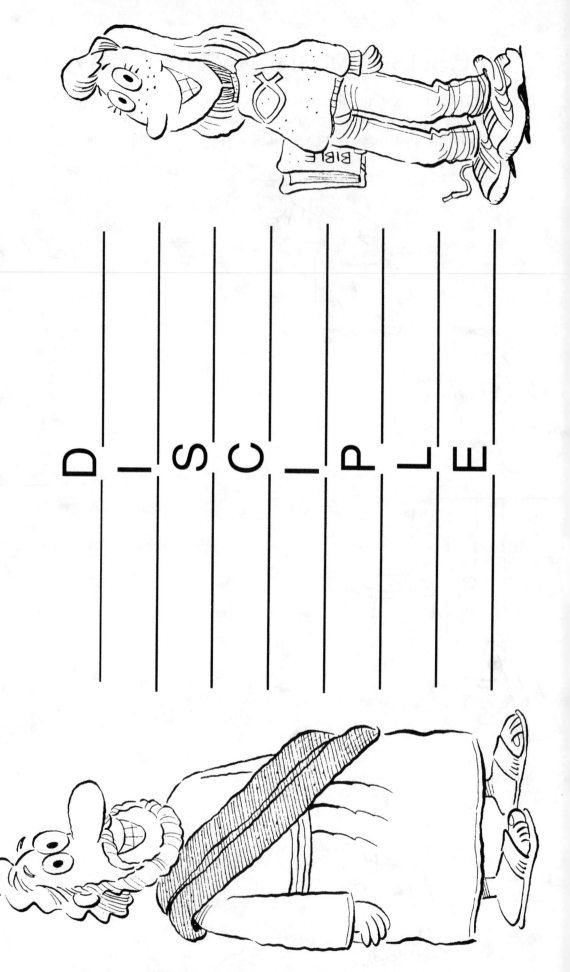

God Loves Us Like . . .

. . . mothers love babies. Draw a baby in the mother's arms.

. . . mother eagles love baby eagles. Draw the baby eagles in the nest.

. . . daddy elephants love baby elephants. Draw the baby elephant.

Advanced King Word Search

Look up these Bible verses. In each verse you will find one or more words that refer to a king—specifically in most verses to the kingship of God and Jesus. Find the words in the puzzle and explain to a friend what each one tells us about Jesus.

You should find 13 words.

Hebrews 1:3b
2 Corinthians 8:9
James 2:8
Psalm 103:19 (3 words)
Genesis 17:1
Matthew 27:29
Exodus 15:7
1 Timothy 6:15
Matthew 9:6
Psalm 22:28a
1 Chronicles 16:29b

The "empty tomb"

is one symbol that reminds us that Jesus is alive. However, it was not the empty tomb that convinced the disciples that Jesus was alive. It was not the empty tomb that helped them to understand. The disciples began to understand what Jesus had been teaching them would happen when Jesus appeared to them after the Resurrection.

Read Matthew 28:8-10. Then find *Jesus' words* to Mary Magdalene and the other Mary in the word search. (*Note:* Some of the answers are in more than one place!)

```
G R B M W I L L Y L E E
A N D R E S E E L T M T
N F E B O O H J O D G T
D G R E E T I N G S E Y
H O L A L O H T H E R E
D M T H I E T E L L W R
R M Y O G D N I R A L I
G W T S A S L N D S W L
H O Y G A A G R W E T D
T W R E G G O O M H S R
```

Now, choose a friend to work with. Read each of these stories about Jesus appearing to someone after the Resurrection. Find out:

❁ *Who* Jesus appeared to   ❁ *How* they recognized Jesus

Luke 24:13-35   Who? _____

How? _____

_____

John 20:24-29   Who? _____

How? _____

_____

John 21:1-11   Who? _____

How? _____

_____

Copyright © 2003 Abingdon Press. Permission is granted for the original purchaser to reproduce this activity for use in a local church setting.
Art: Brenda Gilliam, © 1998 Abingdon Press.

I Can Witness!

Decorate your visor. Then wear it to tell others about Jesus.

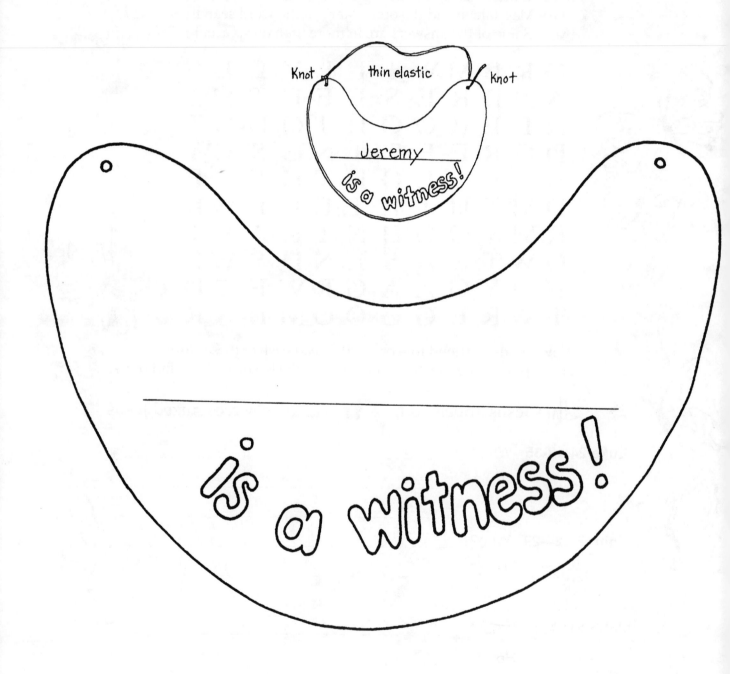

What Do You Remember About Jesus?

Choose words from the mushroom that tell something about Jesus. Write one description on each petal of the flower.

Words on the mushroom: Teacher, Man, Healer, Caring, Savior, Doctor, Selfish, Loves everyone, Kind, Rode a donkey, Woman, Drove a special car

A Change of Heart

1. Color on the back of the paper with red and black crayons. Color to show your feelings when you are angry, sad, or scared.
2. Turn the paper over and cut out the outline of the heart.
3. Turn the heart over. See how the shape of the heart changes the feelings of anger, sadness, and fear into a picture of love.
4. Glue your heart on a sheet of construction paper.
5. Then cut out and add the words "A Change of Heart" to remind you about how Paul's heart was changed when he met Jesus.

Use your Bible (Acts 9:1-9) to help you solve the puzzle.

Down
1. Saul is his Jewish name. But we know him better by his Roman name, _____. (This name is not identified as Roman in the Scripture!)
2. Saul was breathing threats against the Christians and wanted to _____ them.
3. A _____ from heaven flashed around Saul while he was traveling.
5. Saul had to be led by the _____ into the city.
6. Saul heard a _____ call his name.
9. The men who were with him heard the voice, they saw ____ _____. (Two words)

Across
4. Saul was on his way to _____ ____.
7. When Saul got up, he could see _____ ____ even though his eyes were open.
8. When Saul saw the flash of light, he fell to the ____ _____.
10. Saul was without sight and did not eat or drink for _____ days.

Shepherd's Costume

Shepherds wore a cloth headcover for protection from sun and dust; a woolen tunic covered by a mantle, which was also used as a warm blanket; a belt to hold their valuables; and sandals on their feet. They carried a staff to guide the sheep and to use for climbing. Shepherds also carried a rod or heavy stick to use against wild animals. They carried their food, tools, and stones to use with their leather slings in a pouch.

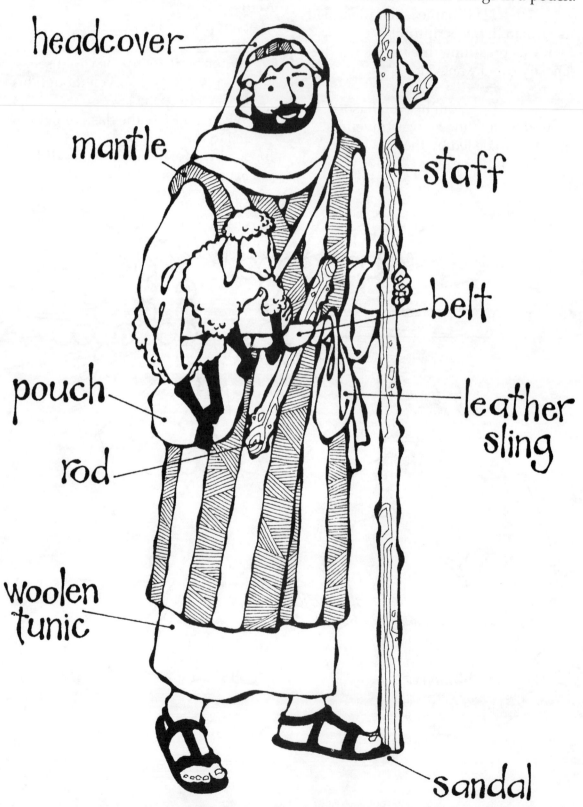

Copyright © 2003 Abingdon Press. Permission is granted for the original purchaser to reproduce this activity for use in a local church setting.
Art: Brenda Gilliam, © 2002 Abingdon Press.

Psalm 23

The Twenty-third Psalm is one of the most beautiful and beloved passages in all of Scripture. One of the reasons for this is the lovely and soothing word pictures it draws, but more important is what those word pictures mean.

He makes me lie down in green pastures

Green pastures are not only pretty but a source of food and nourishment.

He leads me beside still waters

Sheep can't drink from swiftly flowing water, the shepherd must find still water.

He leads me in right paths

A safe path is taken so that danger is avoided and the sheep come to a place of shelter.

The darkest valley

The threat is real, but it is not to be feared because the shepherd will be with the sheep. To make the point even stronger, the psalm writer begins speaking in the first person in this verse.

Your rod and your staff

These are tools the shepherd carried to protect the sheep. The knowledge that God offered the psalm writer protection gave him great comfort.

The last two verses change the image from shepherd to gracious host. The host does the same thing for the guest that the shepherd does for the sheep—offers food and drink, makes the guest comfortable and honored by anointing with oil, and provides shelter and protection.

Copyright © 2003 Abingdon Press. Permission is granted for the original purchaser to reproduce this activity for use in a local church setting.
Art: Charles Jakubowski, © 2002 Abingdon Press.

Use your Bible to complete the crossword puzzle. You can find the names and places in the stories in Acts 11:19-26 and Acts 13:1-5, 14. Read carefully!

Across
3. Barnabas went to this city to find Paul and bring him to Antioch.
5. The followers of Jesus were scattered because of the persecution that resulted in the stoning of this man.
6. Paul and Barnabas went to this city in Cyprus after leaving Seleucia.
7. The Antioch where Paul and Barnabas started the first group called Christians was in Syria. The other Antioch was in this region.
8. The place where believers in Christ were first called Christians was in this city in Syria.

Down
1. When the Jerusalem church heard about the group of believers in Antioch, they sent this man to find out what was happening there.
2. When the Christians scattered from Jerusalem, some men who were from Cyprus and Cyrene came to this city in Syria.
4. In Antioch the believers were first called by this name that is still used today.

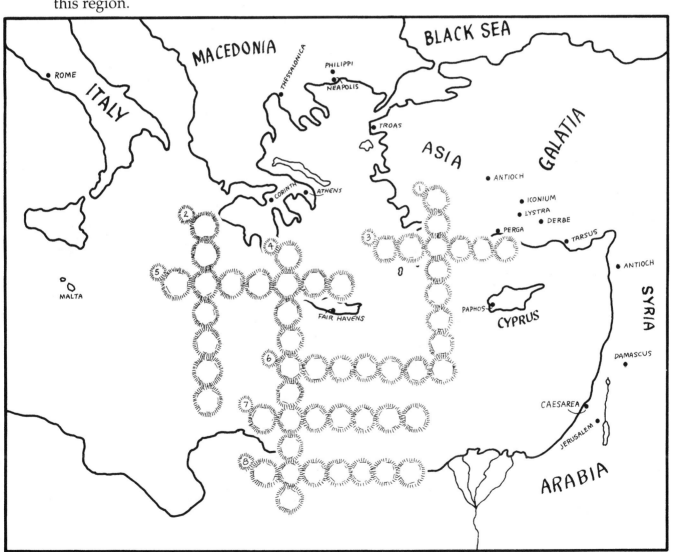

Mail From Across the Centuries

Dear Faithful Ones,

I had heard about Paul before his experience with Jesus Christ on the road to Damascus. I was afraid when I heard that he was coming to our city. But that was nothing compared to the fear I felt when God told me in a vision to go to see Paul and lay my hands on him. But I obeyed God's command. And I am glad I did. Paul has become my brother in Christ, and he has helped many people find God's love in their own lives.

In Christian love,

_____

(Acts 9:10-15)

Dear Sisters and Brothers in Christ,

I was born in a city called Tarsus, but my "second life" began on the road that leads to Damascus. After my conversion, I spent much of my adult life traveling across the lands that surround the Mediterranean Sea. I preached about Jesus. I started new churches and worked to strengthen churches that were already established. I wrote many letters like this one to help the Christians keep their faith strong.

Grace and peace,

_____

(Acts 9:1-6)

Dear Fellow Believers,

Do you know what a mentor is? A mentor is someone who serves as an example, someone who teaches us, someone who listens to us. My mentor when I was young was Paul the Apostle. He reminded me that I should not let anyone look down on me because I was young. He helped me understand that I could be an example for others — perhaps even someone's mentor.

In Christ's service,

_____

(Acts 16:1-3a)

Dear Friends and Fellow Disciples,

I have sometimes been called an encourager. I think that is a good thing. I encouraged the disciples in Jerusalem to accept Paul, even though they were not sure whether to believe he had really been changed by an encounter with Jesus. Later I encouraged Paul to come to Antioch to help with the new church there especially since there were many Gentiles who wanted to hear the good news. I am very glad to say that I was chosen along with Paul to be a missionary. I traveled with him on his first journey.

Yours in the name of Jesus Christ,

_____

(Acts 9:26-28)

Start in the center. Follow the three paths to find ways you can share.

Hard Decisions

Paul and Silas made a hard choice when they stayed in the prison even when the doors were opened. They could have escaped. However, if they had escaped, the jailer would have killed himself. Instead, because of Paul and Silas, the jailer became a Christian. Sometimes choices are not obvious or easy. Read these three situations. Then write what choice you think would be best in each situation.

Danny is loud and silly. He likes to play tricks on everyone, but sometimes he's too rough. Often he does or says hurtful things because he just doesn't think. No one really likes to have him around. Danny's not bad, he's just immature.

You are having a party in a couple of weeks. You plan to invite all the kids from church. Your best friend, though, begs you not to include Danny. What should you do?

_____

_____

You have just moved to a new school. You are shy, and no one is friendly to you except one girl. She went out of her way to be nice to you the first day, and you like her a lot. But today while you were with her, you saw her shoplift a sweater. What should you do?

_____

_____

Your mother has just lost her job. Now money is very tight for your family. You had planned to get a cassette player with headphones, but now that is out of the question. You have a trusted job in the principal's office. You know that there has been a cassette player in your school's lost and found for the last six weeks. No one can prove it isn't yours. What should you do?

_____

_____

Kites

1. Turn a grocery sack so that the bottom is at the top.
2. Decorate the bag with Christian symbols. Use some of the symbols on this page, or add your own.
3. Punch a hole at each of the four corners at the open end of the bag.
4. Tie one end of a piece of yarn (about 18 inches long) in each of the four holes.
5. Pull the ends of the four pieces of yarn together, and tie them in a knot.
6. Attach a longer length of yarn (at least three feet) to the kite by tying it onto the knot.

When you fly your kite, think about the Holy Spirit power that came to the disciples on the Day of Pentecost. Think about how you can use the power of the Holy Spirit that God gives to you.

Tongues of Fire

Winds of the Spirit

Descending Dove

Trinity: Father, Son and Holy Spirit

Cross

Fish

Christian Love

Copyright © 2003 Abingdon Press. Permission is granted for the original purchaser to reproduce this activity for use in a local church setting.
Art: Susan Harrison, © 1998 Abingdon Press.

A Gift From God

Jesus promised his friends that God would send them a gift. God sent this gift to us too. Connect the dots to discover what God sends. Follow the numbers carefully. They may surprise you!

PUT BOW HERE

Belonging

1. Use the pattern to make human figures from construction paper.

2. Use fabric scraps, crayons and markers, yarn, and other craft supplies to dress each figure in a different way.

3. Use the slits in the hands to join the figures into a "belonging line."

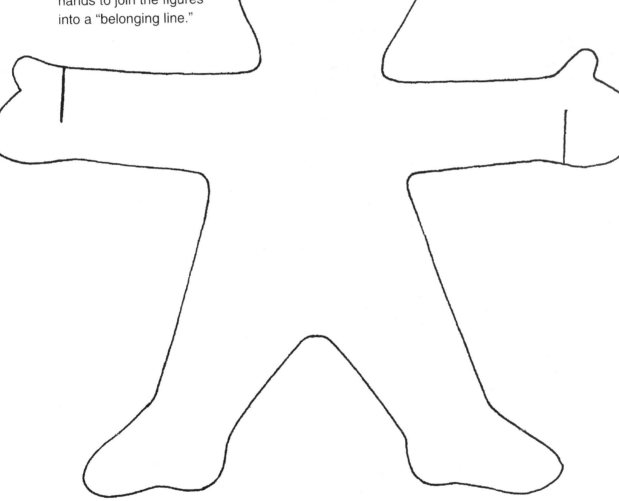

"Belonging Line"

Copyright © 2003 Abingdon Press. Permission is granted for the original purchaser to reproduce this activity for use in a local church setting.
Art: Susan Eaddy (pattern) Florence Davis (figures), © 1994 Cokesbury.

VERSE SEARCH

Cross out all the Zs.
Cross out all the Bs.
Cross out all the Qs.

Read the remaining letters to discover today's Bible verse. Write the words on index cards and use the Word Board to memorize the verse.

NOTICE:

QZBQBYOUQZBQZHAVEBZQGIVENZZZQ
BZTHEMZBZQDOMINIONZQBBZQBOVER
ZBQTHEQBZBQWORKSBBZQOFBZBQBZ
BZBQBZYOURBZBQBZBQZBHANDSBZBZ.

Psalm 8:6a

CONNECT THE DOTS.
When Elijah called upon God, what happened?

Cut apart the picture strips.
Glue them in order on a sheet of construction paper to make a picture.
Color the picture.

Can you tell the story that the picture tells?

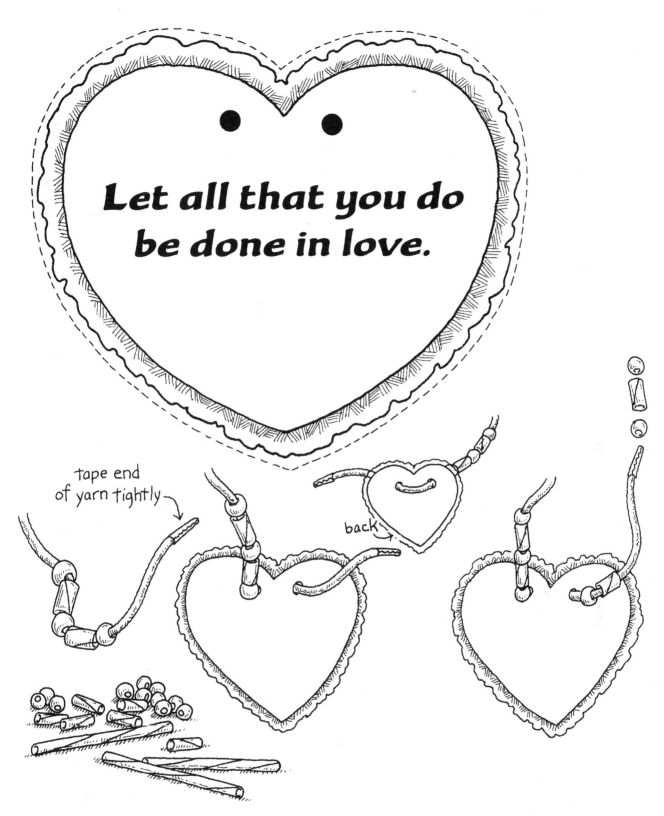

1. Glue the heart on a piece of a used file folder. Then cut it out.
2. Punch the holes at the top of the heart.
3. String the decorations on to the yarn. Alternate using pieces of straw and beads.
4. Thread the yarn through the holes to make a necklace and add more decorations on the other side.
5. Tie the ends of the yarn together. Then wear your necklace to remind yourself and others that acting in loving ways is important.

Good News Bumper Stickers

1. Cut a piece of construction paper into four 3- by 9-inch strips.

2. Draw pictures and write words to tell the good news. (Practice on plain paper first if you wish!)

3. Cut a 4- by 10-inch piece of clear self-adhesive plastic for each bumper sticker.

4. Peel the paper backing from the self-adhesive plastic, leaving the sticky side up. Save the backing.

5. Center the decorated side of your bumper sticker on the sticky side of the clear self-adhesive plastic.

6. Carefully replace the paper backing on the bumper sticker to cover up the sticky edges. Rub your hand over the paper backing.

7. When it is time to attach your bumper sticker, peel the paper off the back to uncover the sticky paper.

Copyright © 2003 Abingdon Press. Permission is granted for the original purchaser to reproduce this activity for use in a local church setting.
Art: Cheryl Mendenhall, © 1994 Cokesbury.

Hand Prayer

Directions: God wants us to pray for others. The Hand Prayer is one way to remember those for whom we should pray. Can you think of anyone who would not fit into one of these groups?

On the back of this paper, trace your own hand and write on it specific prayer concerns.

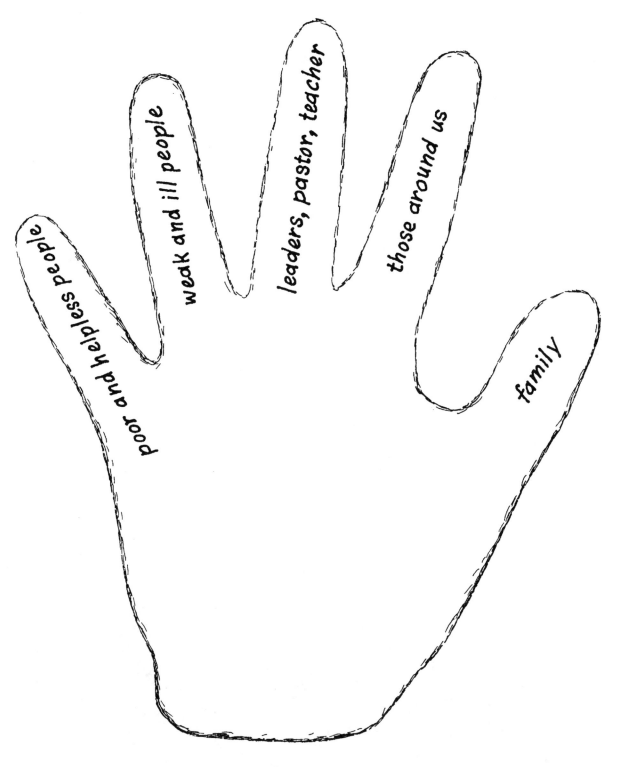

A Bit of Hebrew

Jesus learned to read the Scripture in Hebrew.

Here's a clue. Hebrew and Aramaic are read from right to left. When you read your Bible do you read from right to left or left to right?

שִׁירוּ לַ יהוָה

שִׁיר חָדָשׁ שִׁירוּ

לַיהוָה כָּל־ הָ אֶרֶץ

Key:
לַ	to	כָּל־	all
חָדָשׁ	new	שִׁיר	a song
שִׁירוּ	sing	יהוָה	the Lord
אֶרֶץ	Earth	הָ	the
לַיהוָה	to the Lord		

"God made me,

I'm Special!"

Include Me In!

Break open the boxes to discover what happens when we become children of God through faith.

In the boxes
1. Cross out the first letter of each three-letter word.
2. Remove all the double *E*'s.
3. Mark out all the double consonants.
4. Eliminate all the *W*'s and *M*'s.
5. Scratch off all the *A*'s.
6. Delete the last letter in each five-letter word.
7. Get rid of all the *V*'s.

Now circle all the letters that remain. Unscramble them to make a three-letter word that will complete the Bible verse. Check your answer in your Bible.

Peaceful Child of God Banner

Color the child to look like you, cut it out, and glue it to a piece of construction paper. Decorate the T-shirt anyway you like. Glue it on your child. Hang your banner where it will remind you that you are a peaceful child of God.

"I am a Peaceful child of God"

Copyright © 2003 Abingdon Press. Permission is granted for the original purchaser to reproduce this activity for use in a local church setting.
Art: Nancy Munger, © 2002 Abingdon Press.

Search for Meaning

Fill in the blanks and answer the questions to discover the words and phrases hidden in the word search puzzle.

1. A Christian is a person who B _ _ _ _ _ _ _ in J _ _ _ _.

2. A Christian has the qualities taught and demonstrated by Jesus. See Galatians 5:22-23.

3. Jesus followers were first called Christians in _____. (Acts 11:26)

4. Christians left Jerusalem because they faced _____. (Acts 11:19)

5. _____ and _____ spent one year teaching believers in the city where Jesus' followers were first called Christians. (Acts 11)

6. A Christian should always S _ _ V _ C H _ _ _ _ and try to B _ _ _ M _ _ _ K _ C _ R _ _ T.

Be careful. Words can go in any direction, and several incorrect answers have been hidden as well!

```
A B E C O M E L I K E C H R I S T H G J
T M E J K U W O Y O W B N T R I S A U O
E N D L E A E B L L Y C H W F B R K H
F T P B I P H N P W G I D W A M E M L N
G E N T L E N E S S E R Z I V C I S A I
U P R U S T V J A O F V T K N N H K Z H
W E I E M E O E T D I H W E I J O Y I S
I A T A G R S D S M F B I M U E L N N E
B C E E E H H S E U P T Y S S R C F E R
G E S W P C U R L J A E K U T U O A S D
I J O T O S M N M P I S E D Z S U B S E
Z E R I J U E T S D H N G L U A S M M T
E V T S I S G E U R E V O L Q L E Z C H
Y N G Y S T W C N E J K P H P E O K I W
A B O G E N E R O S I T Y O A M Y I O E
D I O A D M U B K M Y E G E M S A N A B
I G S R B A R N A B A S E T E U Q D W C
R E Q U W R K G P S I A O J O W D N H P
E S O E S E L F C O N T R O L N N E S S
I H E N V E W N Q A S I Q E Y A T S B T
K J P B U K J A N H S C E G U J E S E F
S P E R S E C U T I O N H T E S C G R E
C M G A K S A W R T S I R H C E V R E S
```

Musical Instruments Then and Now

Color the instruments from Bible times one color; instruments from today another; and instruments that were used in Bible times that we still use today a third color.

Jesus taught that . . .

A. neighbors are those who help one another.

B. God is always willing to forgive.

C. God loves each one of us in a special way and knows when we need help.

D. some people will hear and do what Jesus teaches. Other people will not listen and will not do what Jesus teaches.

E. knowing God is worth more than everything else we have.

The Lost Sheep
Luke 15: 3-7

The Forgiving Father
Luke 15: 11-24

The Sower and the Seed
Mark 4: 3-9, 14-20

The Good Samaritan
Luke 10: 29-37

The Pearl of Great Price
Matthew 13: 45-46

Learning From Jesus

Every day Jesus was busy teaching the crowds of people who came to hear him. Jesus often told stories to answer the questions the people asked. One day when Jesus was alone with some of his closest followers, they asked him, "Why do you teach everyone in parables?"

Jesus answered, "It is not easy for people who do not understand the love of God to understand the message that I have come to teach. I use parables to put the message in words that will have meaning for them. It is easier for people to understand what the kingdom of God is like when I compare the kingdom to the things they know. The people understand what happens when a farmer sows seeds. When they hear the comparison, they will be able to understand what it means to hear the message of God's love."

People also learned from Jesus by watching the things he did. For example, one evening Jesus and his disciples started across the Sea of Galilee so that they could rest on the other side. Jesus was tired, and he fell asleep in the back of the boat.

While Jesus slept, a storm began to rock the boat with big waves and strong winds. The disciples were afraid, but Jesus continued to sleep. Finally the disciples woke Jesus up and said, "Teacher, don't you care if we all drown?"

Jesus spoke to the winds. "Peace! Be still, storm!" he said. And the winds stopped. All was calm once again.

Then Jesus turned to his disciples. "Why were you afraid?" he asked. "Didn't you trust me? Have you no faith?"

That night the disciples learned about Jesus' power. And they learned a little more about Jesus' love.

Once when Jesus was visiting in the home of Mary and Martha, Mary sat at Jesus' feet and listened to his stories. She wanted to learn everything she could from Jesus.

Martha loved Jesus too. She wanted to sit and listen to Jesus but she thought, *Jesus is our guest. I must prepare food for him to eat.*

Soon Martha became upset because Mary was not helping her. She had so much to do! Finally she complained to Jesus. "Lord, don't you care that Mary has left me to do all the work? Tell her to help me!"

Jesus said, "Martha, you worry too much about many things. Mary has chosen to listen to me and learn from me. Do not try to take her away from her learning." From Jesus' words Martha learned that although she needed to provide food for her guest, she also needed to find time to learn from Jesus' teaching.

Based on Mark 4:10, 33-41; Luke 10:38-42

Compare the Lord's Prayer as it is written in four versions of Luke 11:2-4.

How would you write your own version of the Lord's Prayer in words that have meaning for you?

The King James Version

Our Father which art in heaven,
Hallowed be thy name.
Thy kingdom come.
Thy will be done, as in heaven,
   so in earth.
Give us day by day our daily bread.
And forgive us our sins; for we also
   forgive every one that is indebted
   to us.
And lead us not into temptation;
   but deliver us from evil.

The Good News Version

Father:
   May your holy name be honored;
   may your Kingdom come.
   Give us day by day the food
     we need.
   Forgive us our sins,
     for we forgive everyone
     who does us wrong.
   And do not bring us to hard testing.

The Contemporary English Version

Father, help us to honor your name.
Come and set up your kingdom.
Give us each day the food we need.
Forgive our sins,
   as we forgive everyone who has done
     wrong to us.
And keep us from being tempted.

The New Revised Standard Version

Father, hallowed be your name.
   Your kingdom come.
   Give us each day our daily bread.
   And forgive us our sins,
     for we ourselves forgive
     everyone indebted to us.
   And do not bring us to the
     time of trial.

The Lord's Prayer is also in Matthew 6:9-13.
Read that version in whatever Bibles you have.
How is it alike or different from the versions in Luke?

Prayer Book

1
A Morning Prayer

Good morning, God,
Thank you for the rest I got during the night.
Be with me through the day.
Help me find ways to share your love with other people. Amen.

2
Prayer Before a Meal

O Great Creator,
Thank you for providing food for our table. As we eat, help us remember those who grew, harvested, and prepared this food. Bless those people who do not have enough to eat, and show us ways to help them. Amen.

3
A Prayer for Obedience

Dear God,
Please help me be good,
As I know I should.

When it's hard to obey,
Please show me the way.
Amen.

4
A Prayer for Those I Love

Loving God,
Bless my family and friends. Help us be kind and caring to each other.

Thank you for sending your Son to teach us how to be more loving.
Amen.

Prayer Book

5

A Prayer for When I'm Scared or Sad

(sung to tune of "Twinkle, Twinkle, Little Star")

When I'm scared
Or when I'm blue
I know I can talk to you.
Give me peace
And make me calm.
Please be with me all day long.
When I'm scared
Or when I'm blue
I know I can talk to you.

6

6. Finger Prayer

Thumb: When I put a clenched hand to my chest, my thumb is the closest to my heart, so I remember to pray for my family and friends.
Pointer Finger: I pray for those who point me to the truth.
Middle Finger: My middle finger is my tallest finger, so I pray for leaders.
Ring Finger: The ring finger is the weakest finger. I pray for those who are weak or sick.
Pinky: My pinky is the smallest finger. I pray for people who cannot help themselves (such as people who are affected by war).

7

The ABC Prayer

This prayer helps us remember to include the following things as we pray:

A = Adoration—praise to God
B = Blessings for those I know and for me
C = Confession—admitting to God the wrong things I have done
D = Desires of my heart—I tell God what I really, really want.
E = Everyone—I pray that everyone will come to know Jesus.

8

A Nighttime Prayer

O God of Rest,
Thank you for the day that is ending.
Thank you for tomorrow and all the days to come.
Help me to rest peacefully, knowing that you are always near.
Amen.

Copyright © 2003 Abingdon Press. Permission is granted for the original purchaser to reproduce this activity for use in a local church setting.
© 2000 Abingdon Press.

1. Carefully outline the letters with glue.

2. Completely cover the glue with glitter.

3. Allow the glue to dry; then shake off the excess glitter.

4. Glue the page to a sheet of construction paper.

5. Punch holes and add yarn to hang the picture.

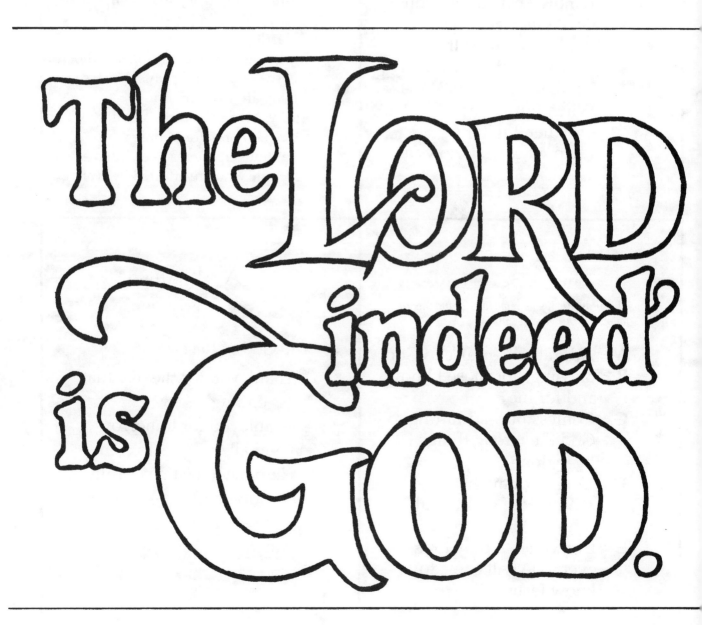

Growing Up

Circle the words below that name ways you can reach out to other people to show them that you care about them.

Compliment	Interact	Ignore	Reject
Speak	Care	Help	Give
Disapprove	Love	Hate	Tattle
Include	Frown	Accept	
Smile	Share	Tease	

Can you add some other words to circle? _____ _____

Fill in all the spaces in the letters below that contain *O*'s. Who does Jesus love and want us to reach out to? _____

```
I YQ J H Y T E C W E T U F C D E W C S W T F E C R D F E W T Y G V E A L Q P J
O O O B O Z A R O X O O O I O O O W S B O B W V O Q O O O Y O U J P O K O O O K
O L B X O V P F O M O K W D O E O C W T R O G O R F O T O B O O U K O M O G H N
O O Y Q N O K O A Z O O L X O O O Y R V K K O Q H Q O S O X O L O E O I O O P G
O Z D M C O N O B J O B E F O I E O C I H W O H X E O A O A O G A O O F O G Z J
O O O P A U O K M T O O O Z O K J L O J R H O B I D O O O U O S R G O C O O O F
D Y N V L Y U Y P N F Y M K N Q L J C V A U L G F Z W V R F D H P S K I H D L Z
```

Use a red crayon to circle the thing you did when you were a baby. Use a blue crayon to circle the thing you did when you were two years old. Use a green crayon to circle the things you do now. Use a purple crayon to circle the thing you will be able to do when you are older.

Copyright © 2003 Abingdon Press. Permission is granted for the original purchaser to reproduce this activity for use in a local church setting.
Art: Susan Harrison, © 1997 Abingdon Press.

Following each description of a prophet you will see three pictures. Circle the picture that goes with the words. Who is the prophet?

Jeremiah was a prophet.

A prophet hears God's word.

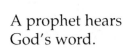  

A prophet helps people understand God's laws.

A prophet helps people understand the Bible.

A prophet tells people about God.

A prophet obeys God.

INVITE A FRIEND TO SUNDAY SCHOOL

Jeremiah shared God's word even though he was just a boy. You can share God's word too, even though you are still young, by inviting a friend to Sunday school. Make a special invitation to give to a friend.

MAKE A HEART PERSON

SUPPLIES: construction paper, scissors, markers or crayons, glue

1. Cut out a big heart to be the body. Write your invitation on this heart. Be sure to include the name of your church and the time of Sunday school on it.

2. Cut out a slightly smaller heart for the head. Decorate it with yarn or narrow strips of construction paper for hair, if you like.

3. Cut out four small hearts for hands and feet.

4. Glue the head and hands and feet to the body with strips of construction paper folded in an accordion fold.

5. Share it with a friend this week.

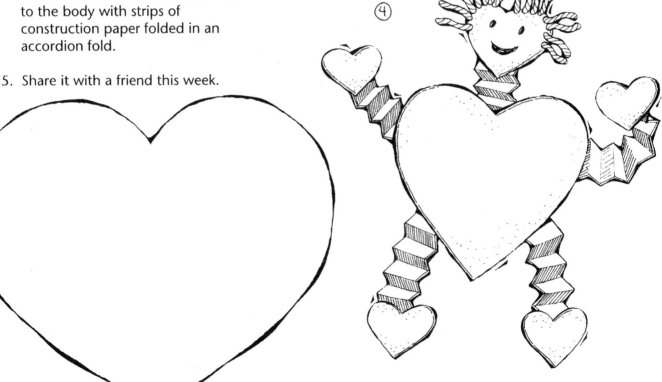

Copyright © 2003 Abingdon Press. Permission is granted for the original purchaser to reproduce this activity for use in a local church setting.
Art: Susan Harrison, © 2001 Abingdon Press.

Fill in the Face

Jeremiah had a lot of different feelings. Sometimes he was sad because the people would not listen to him. Sometimes he was angry because they would not listen. Sometimes he was happy because God gave him a good message to deliver. How would you feel when these things happened? Draw a face showing how you would feel.

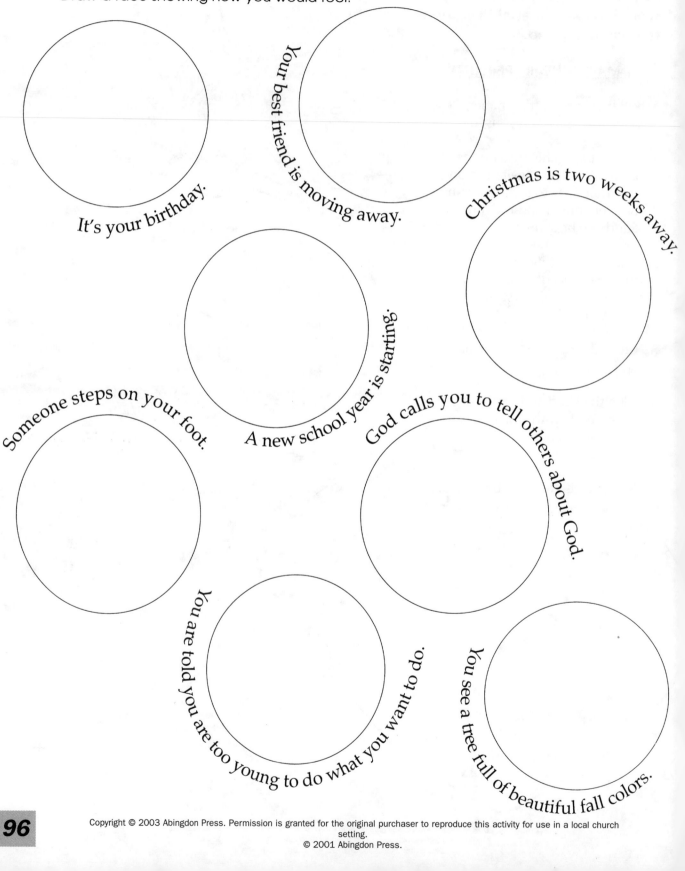

- It's your birthday.
- Your best friend is moving away.
- Christmas is two weeks away.
- Someone steps on your foot.
- A new school year is starting.
- God calls you to tell others about God.
- You are told you are too young to do what you want to do.
- You see a tree full of beautiful fall colors.

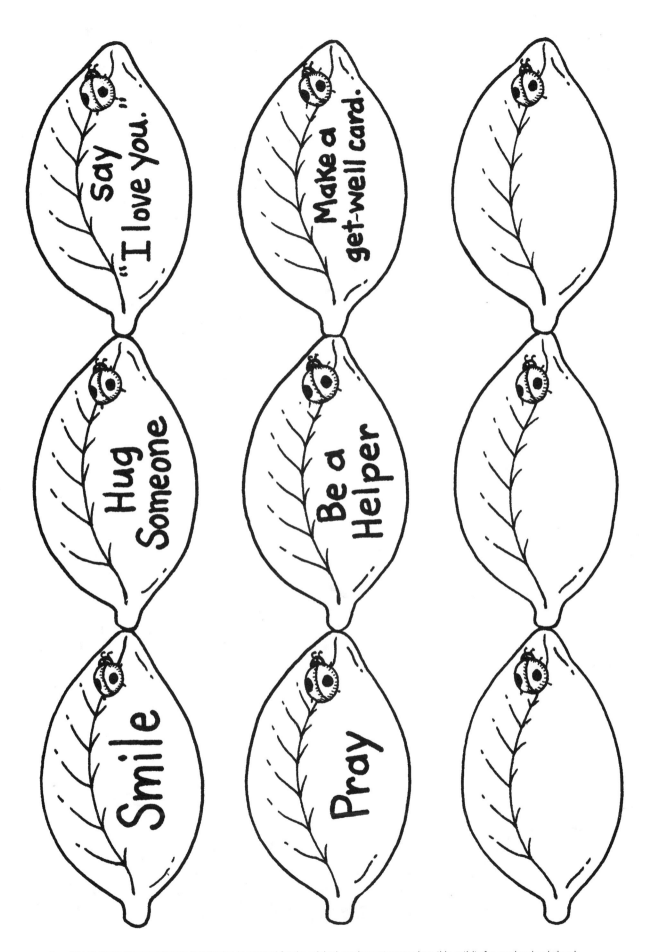

How do you spend your allowance?
Make a pie chart to show what your money does.

How much do you

save?

give to the church?

spend on gifts?

spend on school supplies?

spend on pizza, gum, and candy?

spend on other things? (List them.)

_____

_____

_____

_____

_____

For

Let us give praise to God!

For

Let us give praise to God!

Because

Let us give praise to God!
Let the whole world praise Almighty God!

**Would you rather go swimming or go to the zoo?
Make a choice. Then follow the path that gets you
where you want to be.**

Paul told Timothy to be an example for others in speech, in how he acted, and in love and faith. Paul expected Timothy to set an example both for people his own age or younger and for those who were older.

You can be an example to others too. Write some ideas about how you can set a good example for others. If you want to, draw a picture to go with your words.

I can set an example by **How I Act** by...

I can set an example in **Speech** by...

I can set an example in **Faith and Love** by...

Use your Bible to finish the story from the Book of Jeremiah.

Then when the words are placed in order in the correct shapes in the puzzle, God's message will show up in the row of large boxes from top to bottom.

The Lord said to Jeremiah, "You shall speak whatever I _____ you. *(1:7c)* I have appointed you a _____ to the nations." *(1:5c)*

Jeremiah said, "Lord, I do not know how to _____." *(1:6)* But the Lord answered, "You shall go to all to whom I _____ you." *(1:7b)*

It was in the thirteenth year of King Josiah's _____ *(1:2)* that the Lord said to Jeremiah, "Do not be afraid . . . , for I am with you to _____ _____." *(1:8)*

The Lord _____ Jeremiah's _____ , and said, "I have put my _____ in your mouth." *(1:9)*

Jeremiah stood in the court of the Lord's house and spoke to those who came to _____. *(26:2)*

He said, "_____ your ways and your doings, and _____ the voice of the Lord. *(26:13)* For in truth the Lord sent me to _____ all these words in your ears." *(26:15b)*

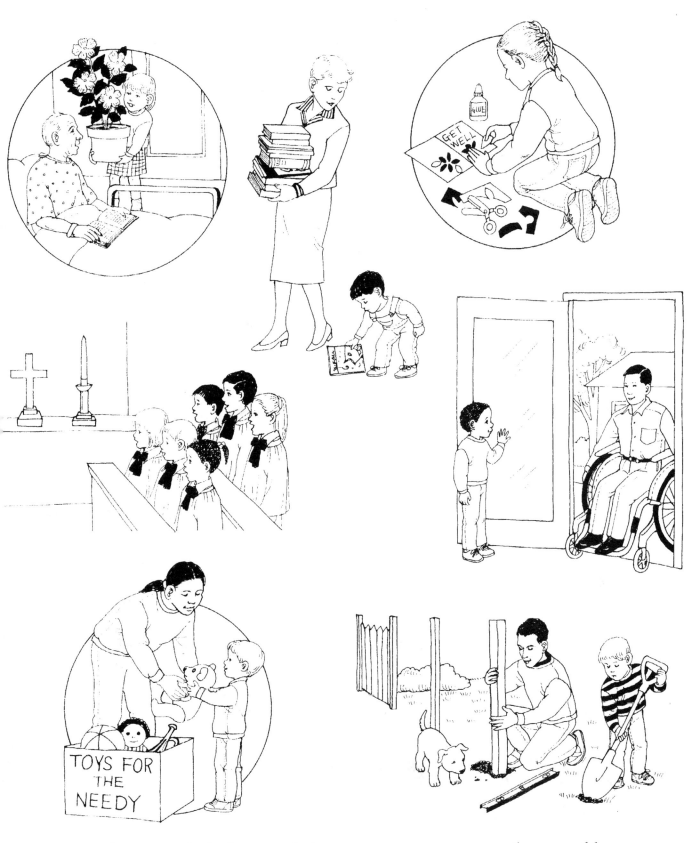

1. Cut out the locket and the circle.
2. Fold the locket in half so that the tree is on the inside.
3. Glue the circle on the front of the locket.
4. Decorate around the words on the front of the locket with markers, with glue and glitter, or with whatever craft supplies you choose.
5. Open the locket, and tape one mustard seed in the circle at the trunk of the tree.
6. Tape the center of a piece of yarn (about 22 inches long) across the fold.
7. Tie the ends of the yarn to complete the necklace. Adjust the length of the yarn to fit around your neck.
8. Close the locket, and crease the tape at the fold.

Locket

Pocket Card

Copyright © 2003 Abingdon Press. Permission is granted for the original purchaser to reproduce this activity for use in a local church setting.
Art: Barbara Upchurch, © 1998 Abingdon Press.

DECODE THE MESSAGE

Word Search

Read 2 Timothy 3:16-17.

Find these words in the puzzle below:
scripture, inspired, God, useful, teaching, good, belongs, everyone, training, correction, reproof, work.

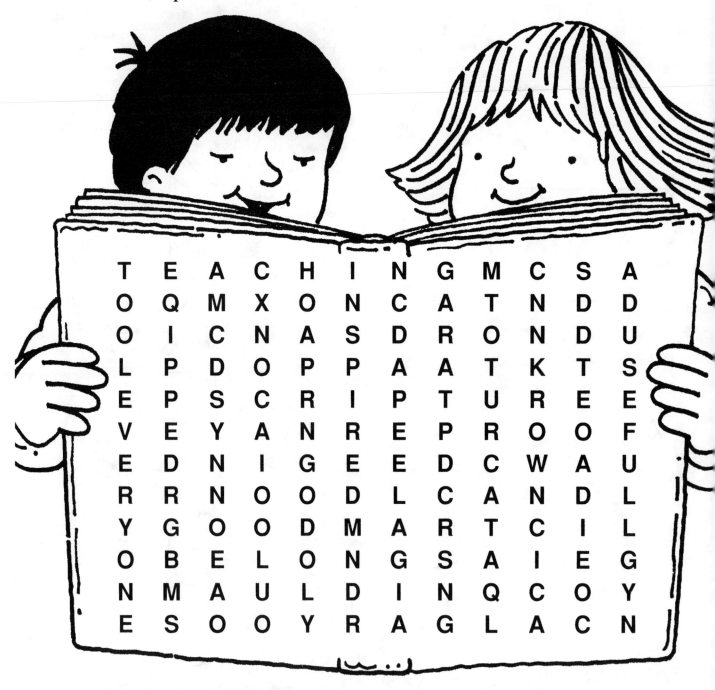

```
T E A C H I N G M C S A
O Q M X O N C A T N D D
O I C N A S D R O N D U
L P D O P P A T K T S
E P S C R I P T U R E E
V E Y A N R E P R O F
E D N I G E E D C W A U
R R N O O D L C A N D L
Y G O O D M A R T C I L
O B E L O N G S A I E G
N M A U L D I N Q C O Y
E S O O Y R A G L A C N
```

Timothy learned from Paul that there are four important uses for the Bible. List them on the back of this page and talk with a friend or teacher about the meaning of each.

I Can Show Respect

Circle the pictures that show people treating others with respect.
How can you show respect to someone this week?

My Sunday school teacher tells good stories.

No, you can't have it!

I don't like to stay on the driveway.

I help my dad with supper.

I like to help keep my town clean.

I want to go first!

Where Timothy Helped to Carry the Good News

Read these Scriptures to find some of the places where Timothy went as a missionary helper with Paul. Mark on the map with a red pencil or crayon those places where Timothy went, either alone or with Paul.

Acts 18:1-5
1 Thessalonians 3:1-2
Acts 19:22
Acts 17:13-14

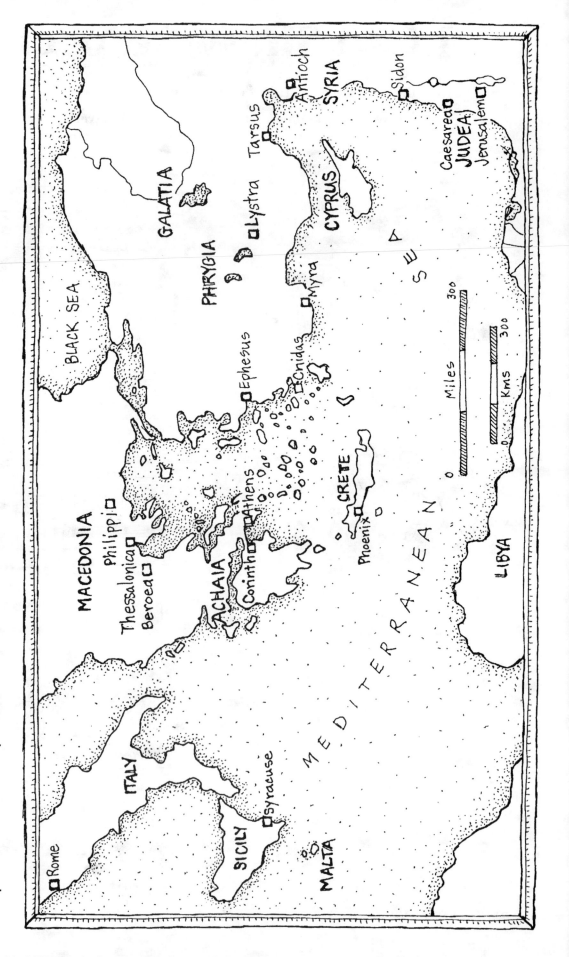

What can you find in the tree?

Read a story about what Jesus found in a tree
one day in Luke 19:1-9.

1. Cut out the card on the solid line.
2. Fold on the broken line (- - -) so that the outline of the child is on the outside.
3. Cut out the child along the solid line. Be careful! Don't cut the space at the ends of the arms!
4. Open the card flat again.
5. Fold on the dotted line (. . .) so that the child outline shows.
6. Pull the figure forward and make a crease at the end of each arm to help the figure "pop out" from the page.
7. Then fold from left to right to make a card. The "pop out" will fold forward. The cover should be on the front.

Copyright © 2003 Abingdon Press. Permission is granted for the original purchaser to reproduce this activity for use in a local church setting.
Art: Megan Jeffery, © 1997 Abingdon Press.

Copyright © 2003 Abingdon Press. Permission is granted for the original purchaser to reproduce this activity for use in a local church setting.
Art: Shelley Dietrichs/Publishers' Graphics, © 1997 Abingdon Press.

A FAMILY PEACE PRAYER

Dear God,
We pray this prayer for family peace.
Help us to think kind thoughts and say kind words,
Help us to listen to one another and to give good advice,
Help us to make our meals and all of our times together times of peace.
We pray in the name of Jesus,
Who said, "My peace I leave with you."
Amen.

Index

Lectionary, Year C

First Sunday of Advent	3, 4
Second Sunday of Advent	5, 6
Third Sunday of Advent	7, 8
Fourth Sunday of Advent	9, 10
Christmas	11, 12
First Sunday After Christmas	13, 14
Epiphany	15, 16
Baptism of the Lord	17, 18
Second Sunday After Epiphany	19, 20
Third Sunday After Epiphany	21, 22
Fourth Sunday After Epiphany	23, 24
Fifth Sunday After Epiphany	25, 26
Sixth Sunday After Epiphany	27, 28
Seventh Sunday After Epiphany	29, 30
Eighth Sunday After Epiphany	31, 32
Transfiguration	33, 34
First Sunday in Lent	35, 36
Second Sunday in Lent	37, 38
Third Sunday in Lent	39, 40
Fourth Sunday in Lent	41, 42
Fifth Sunday in Lent	43, 44
Sixth Sunday in Lent	45, 46
Passion/Palm Sunday	47, 48, 49
Easter	50, 51
Second Sunday of Easter	52, 53
Third Sunday of Easter	54, 55
fourth Sunday of Easter	56, 57
Fifth Sunday of Easter	58, 59
Sixth Sunday of Easter	60, 61, 62
Seventh Sunday of Easter	63, 64
Pentecost	65, 66
Trinity Sunday	67, 68
Sunday Between May 29 and June 4	69, 70
Sunday Between June 5 and 11	71, 72
Sunday Between June 12 and 18	73, 74
Sunday Between June 19 and 25	75, 76
Sunday Between June 26 and July 2	77, 78
Sunday Between July 3 and 9	79, 80
Sunday Between July 10 and 16	81, 82
Sunday Between July 17 and 2	83, 84
Sunday Between July 24 and 30	85, 86
Sunday Between July 31 and August 6	87, 88
Sunday Between August 7 and 13	89, 90
Sunday Between August 14 and 20	91, 92
Sunday Between August 21 and 27	93, 94
Sunday Between August 28 and September 3	95, 96
Sunday Between September 4 and 10	97, 98
Sunday Between September 11 and 17	99, 100
Sunday Between September 18 and 25	101, 102
Sunday Between September 25 and October 1	103, 104
Sunday Between October 2 and 8	105, 106
Sunday Between October 9 and 15	107, 108
Sunday Between October 16 and 22	109, 110
Sunday Between October 23 and 29	111, 112
Sunday Between October 30 and November 5	113, 114
Sunday Between November 6 and 12	115, 116
Sunday Between November 13 and 19	117, 118
Christ the King	119, 120

Scripture

Old Testament

Genesis 17:1	48
Exodus 15:7	48
Exodus 20:12	34
1 Chronicles 16:29b	48
Psalm 4:8	10

Psalm 8	32
Psalm 8:6a	68
Psalm 9:1-2	32
Psalm 22:28a	48
Psalm 23	57
Psalm 71:14	10
Psalm 92:1-4	32
Psalm 100:1-5	48
Psalm 103:19	48
Psalm 103:20	10
Proverbs 3:5-6	34
Isaiah 40:29	14
Jeremiah 1:2	104
Jeremiah 1:5c	104
Jeremiah 1:8	104
Jeremiah 1:9	104
Jeremiah 26:2	104
Jeremiah 26:13	104
Jeremiah 26:15b	104

New Testament

Matthew 4:1-4	34
Matthew 6:9-13	85
Matthew 7:5-7	34
Matthew 9:6	48
Matthew 13:45-46	81
Matthew 27:29	48
Matthew 28:2	10
Matthew 28:8-10	51
Mark 1:1-3	40
Mark 4:10, 33-41	81
Luke 1:1-4	40
Luke 1:26	10
Luke 2:9-10	10
Luke 4:16-19	34
Luke 5:11b	25
Luke 6:27-36	30
Luke 10:38-42	83
Luke 11:2-4	85
Luke 15:3-7	81
Luke 15:10	10
Luke 16:22	10
Luke 24:13-35	51
John 1:1-5	40
John 8:12	34
John 13:34	34
John 15:11	14
John 16:24	14
John 20:24-29	51
John 21:1-11	51
Acts 9:1-9	55
Acts 9:10-15	61
Acts 9:26-28	61
Acts 11:19-26	59
Acts 13:1-5, 14	59
Acts 16:1-3a	61
Acts 17:13-14	112
Acts 18:1-5	112
Acts 19:22	112
Romans 15:13	14
1 Corinthians 13:4a	23
2 Corinthians 8:9	48
Galatians 3:28	76
1 Thessalonians 3:1-2	112
1 Timothy 6:15	48
2 Timothy 3:16-17	110
Ephesians 6:10	14
Hebrews 1:3b	48
Hebrews 1:14	10
Hebrews 13:1	14
James 2:8	48
James 4:11	34
Colossians 1:16	10
Colossians 3:15	14
1 John 4:7	14
Revelation 10:1	10

Puzzle Answers

Gifts for Jesus

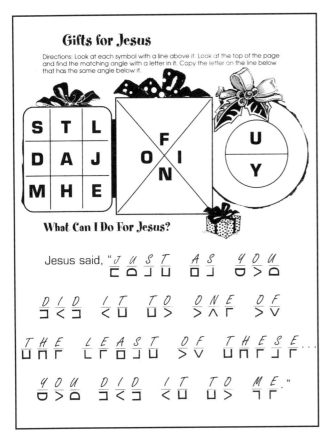

What Can I Do For Jesus?

Jesus said, "JUST AS YOU DID IT TO ONE OF THE LEAST OF THESE... YOU DID IT TO ME."

Angles on Angels

Here are some facts from the Bible about angels. Find and read each verse and fill in the blanks. The correct answers are scrambled after each verse. How is your angel knowledge?

Psalm 103:20 Bless the LORD, O you his angels, you __mighty__ ones who do his __bidding__. gyhmit ddgiibn

Revelation 10:1 And I saw another __mighty__ angel coming down from heaven, wrapped in a cloud, with a __rainbow__ over his head; his face was like the __sun__, and his legs like __pillars__ of fire. tihmgy brownia uns lraplis

Colossians 1:16 For in him all things in __heaven__ and on __earth__ were created, things __visible__ and __invisible__ ... all things have been created through him and for him. [This verse is talking about Jesus, and *everything* includes angels.] venahe rehat iibIsev iiibsvenl

Luke 16:22 The poor man died and was __carried__ away by the angels to be with __Abraham__. [Angels take us to heaven.] ridarce bhmarAa

Luke 15:10 Just so, I tell you, there is __joy__ in the __presence__ of the angels of God over one sinner who __repents__. oyj seecnpre glesan perents

Hebrews 1:14 Are not all angels spirits in the divine __service__, sent to __serve__ for the sake of those who are to inherit salvation? crivees vrees

Luke 1:26 In the sixth month the angel Gabriel was __sent__ by God to a town in Galilee called Nazareth. tsen

Luke 2:9-10 Then an angel of the Lord __stood__ before them, and the glory of the Lord shone around them, and they were terrified. But the angel __said__ to them, "Do not be afraid." oodst dsia

Matthew 28:2 And suddenly there was a great earthquake; for an angel of the Lord, __descending__ from heaven, __came__ and __rolled__ back the stone and sat on it. sceeddgnni meac ldelro

Page 8   Page 10

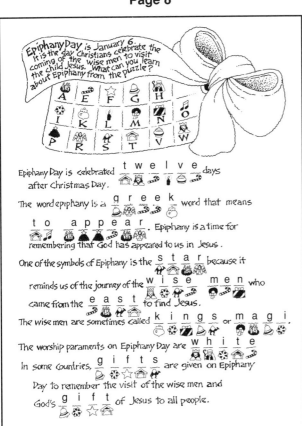

Epiphany Day is celebrated __twelve__ days after Christmas Day.

The word epiphany is a __greek__ word that means __to appear__. Epiphany is a time for remembering that God has appeared to us in Jesus.

One of the symbols of Epiphany is the __star__ because it reminds us of the journey of the __wise men__ who came from the __east__ to find Jesus.

The wise men are sometimes called __kings__ or __magi__.

The worship paraments on Epiphany Day are __white__.

In some countries, __gifts__ are given on Epiphany Day to remember the visit of the wise men and God's __gift__ of Jesus to all people.

Bible Verse Puzzle

	1	2	3	4	5
C	C	U	A	M	H	W
F	F	P	E	N	B	I
G	G	O	S	Y	V	J
K	K	R	T	L	D	X

You are my son,
G3 G1 C1 C2 K1 F2 C3 G3 G2 G1 F3

the beloved, with
K2 C4 F2 F4 F2 K3 G1 G4 F2 K4 C5 F5 K2 C4

you I am well
G3 G1 C1 F5 C2 C3 C5 F2 K3 K3

pleased.
F1 K3 F2 C2 G2 F2 K4

Page 16   Page 18

123

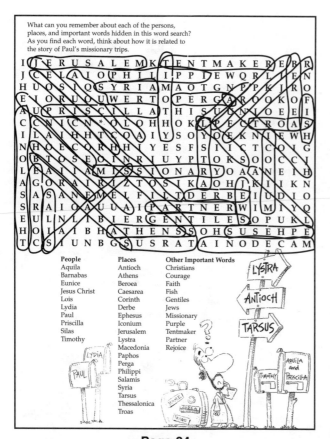

Page 24

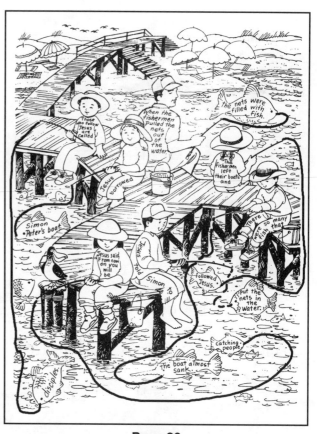

Page 26

Page 30

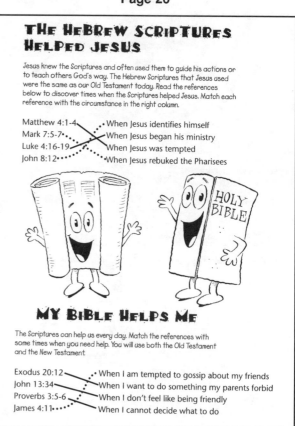

Page 34

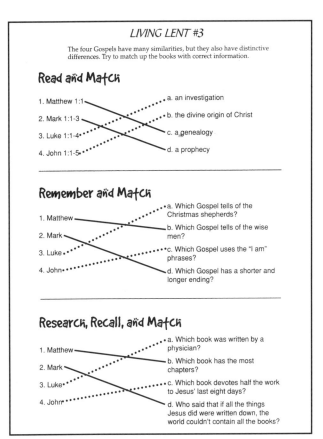

Page 40

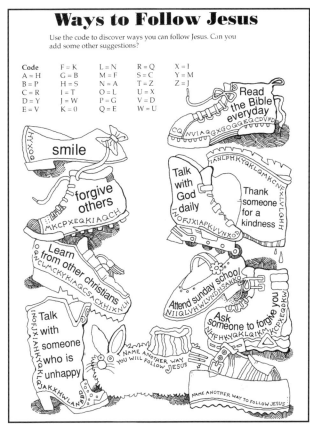

Page 42

Page 46

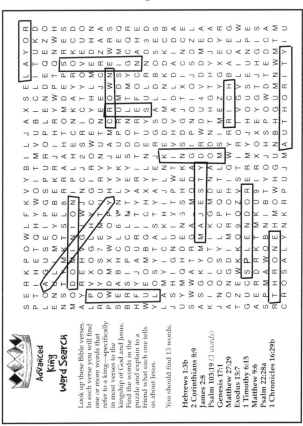

Page 48

125

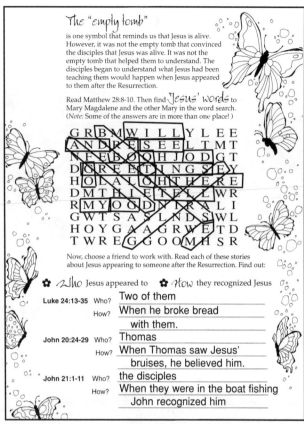

Page 51

Page 55

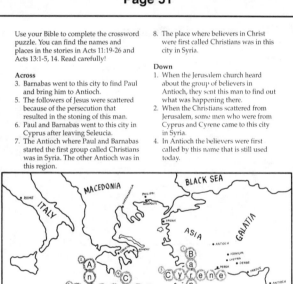

Page 59

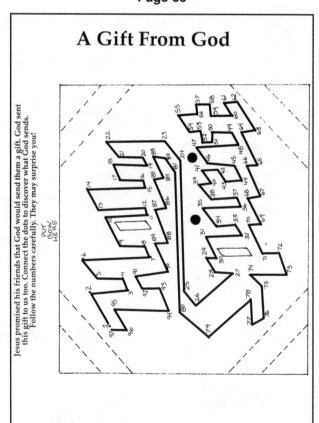

Page 66

Page 68

Page 74

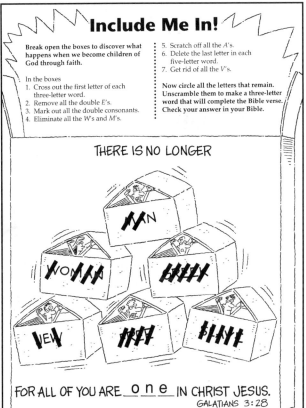

Page 76

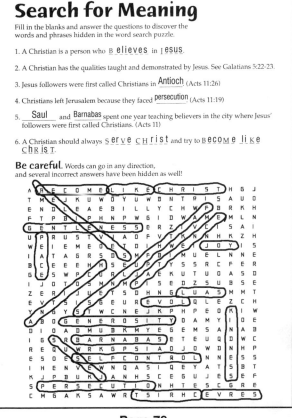

Page 78

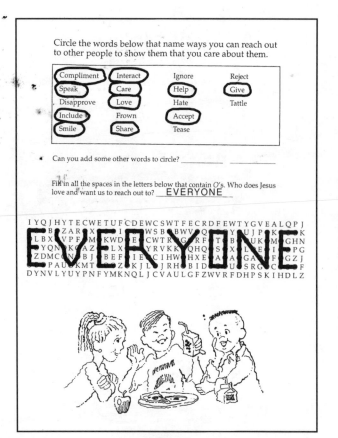

Page 90

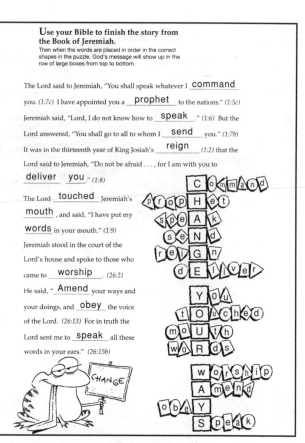

Page 104

Page 106

Page 110

128